MATHS MAGIC

Adding and Subtracting

Written by Wendy Clemson
and David Clemson

LONDON ■ PRINCETON
www.two-canpublishing.com

Published by Two-Can Publishing
43-45 Dorset Street, London W1U 7NA

www.two-canpublishing.com

© Two-Can Publishing 2001

For information on Two-Can books and multimedia,
call (0)20 7224 2440, fax (0)20 7224 7005
or visit our website at http://www.two-canpublishing.com

Created by
act-two
346 Old Street
London EC1V 9RB

Authors: Wendy Clemson and David Clemson

Editor: Penny Smith
Designers: Helen Holmes and Maggi Howells
Illustrators: Andy Peters and Mike Stones
Photographer: Daniel Pangbourne
Pre-press production: Adam Wilde

Two-Can Publishing is a division of Zenith Entertainment plc,
43-45 Dorset Street, London W1U 7NA

Hardback ISBN 1-85434-874-4
Paperback ISBN 1-85434-875-2

Dewey Decimal Classification 513

Hardback 10 9 8 7 6 5 4 3 2 1
Paperback 10 9 8 7 6 5 4 3 2 1

A catalogue record for this book is available
from the British Library.

Colour separation by Colourscan Overseas, Singapore
Printed in Hong Kong

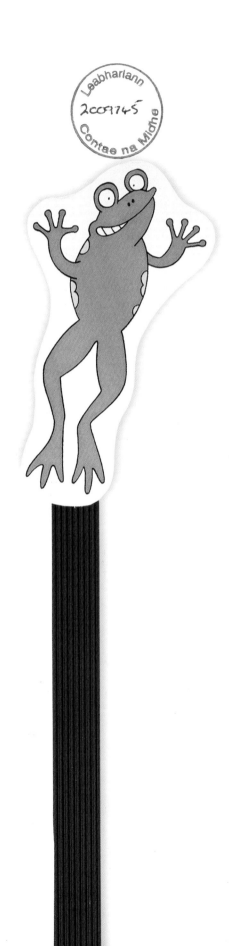

Contents

Sign language

There is a special language that helps you understand adding and subtracting. It's a code of numbers and signs. Explore this space picture and answer the questions to discover how to crack the calculation code!

CODE BREAKER

+ is the sign that means add or plus

− means take away, subtract or minus

= means equals or the same as

So five plus three equals eight can be written 5 + 3 = 8.

1. Count the red planets and blue planets. Now add them together. How do you write this in code?

2. Count the number of white stars, then take away the number of yellow stars. How do you write this in code?

3. Add together the number of rockets and the number of space stations. How do you write this as a calculation?

PROVE IT!

Signs make all the difference in a calculation. The signs on the top shelf tell you that you're adding puppets. One puppet plus two puppets equals three puppets. Can you see how the calculations on the other shelves work?

Balancing numbers

Think of calculations as balancing acts. What is on one side of the equals sign must balance with what is on the other side. It is a bit like the seesaws shown here.

Number track

Here's a nifty gadget to help you add up and take away. It has two parts, a number track and a number jumper. When you want to add, all you have to do is move the jumper in this direction ➔. And when you want to take away, hop the jumper back this way ⬅.

Top tip
Watch out for the + and − signs in a calculation. They tell you in which direction to move your number jumper.

+ ➔

− ⬅

Make a number track and number jumper

YOU WILL NEED
felt pens, coloured card, scissors, glue, sticky tape

1 Copy the outline of the number track below on to card. Ask an adult to help you cut out a slit in the middle. Stick lillypad numbers from 1 to 10 along the bottom.

this is the number track

1   2   3   4   5   6   7

2 To make the number jumper, copy the frog below or draw your own. Cut it out and tape it to a long strip of card. Push the number jumper through the slit in the number track.

3 Now hop to it! Can you find the answer to 4 + 2? Put the number jumper at 4 and jump on 2. You should reach 6 because 4 + 2 = 6. Have fun with more number jumping calculations.

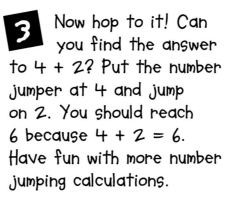

this is the
·········· number jumper

8 9 10

PROVE IT!

Numbers make patterns when you add them together and when you take them away. Look at what happens to the numbers 4, 5 and 9 below. Check the calculations on your number track.

4 + 5 = 9

5 + 4 = 9

9 - 4 = 5

9 - 5 = 4

Number pairs

There are simple calculations, called number pairs, which we use again and again. What's the answer to 3 − 2 or 4 + 1? When you know these kinds of calculations off by heart, you'll be a speedy maths wizard. Play this game to practise taking away numbers up to 10.

Make subtraction bingo cards

YOU WILL NEED
coloured card, ruler, pen, scissors, hat

9-7	6-3	7-4	10-1	7-2
10-7	5-4	8-4	10-6	9-4
9-8	10-4	8-5	4-3	8-2

10-2	3-2	7-5	10-8	9-5
8-6	7-3	6-5	9-2	6-2
10-5	9-6	8-3	10-3	9-3

Copy these baseboards

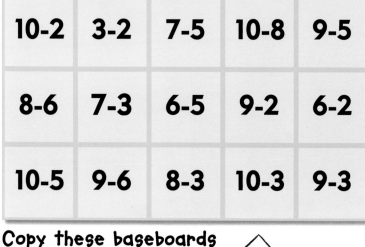

number cards are for covering the squares on the baseboards

1 Copy the yellow baseboard and green baseboard on this page. Make the squares on the baseboards have 5 cm sides.

2 Then make your number cards. You'll need 5 of each of these numbers: 1, 2, 3, 4, 5, 6, 7, 8, 9.

3 Now play the game. You need three people. Two are players. They take a baseboard each. The other person is the caller. She puts the number cards in the hat. Then she picks out one card and calls out the number written on it.

this girl is a player

I'm the caller. I've picked out number 9.

4 Players search their baseboards for a number pair that equals the called-out number. The first to find a match wins the number card and covers the number pair on the baseboard. The first person to completely cover the board is the winner.

Bingo! I'm the winner!

PROVE IT!

There are eight number pairs that add up to seven. Turn the book to look at the petals on the flower and see what they are. How many number pairs can you make that add up to eight, nine and ten?

7 + 0 =
0 + 7 =
6 + 1 =
1 + 6 =
5 + 2 =
2 + 5 =
4 + 3 =
3 + 4 =
7

Two by two

You can save time when you count by adding a number to itself again and again. This farmer is counting sheep two by two. But you can also count in threes, fours, fives, or use even higher numbers.

Picture-addition chart

Use the picture chart on this page to help you count. For ones, add together the balls. For twos add together the pairs of socks. For threes count the prongs on the forks. Use button holes to count in fours and fingers to count in fives. Now solve these picture addition puzzles.

$2 + 2 + 2 + 2 + 2 = ?$

$3 + 3 + 3 = ?$

$5 + 5 + 5 + 5 = ?$

Make your own picture-addition chart for 1 to 10. Draw eggs in a box for number 6, candles on a cake for number 7, legs on a spider for number 8. What else can you use on your chart?

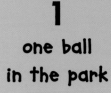

1

+1

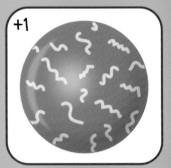

+1

+1

+1

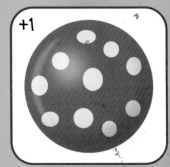

Answers: $2+2+2+2+2=10$ $3+3+3=9$ $5+5+5+5=20$

2
two socks
in a pair

3
three prongs
on a fork

4
four holes
in a button

5
five fingers
on your hand

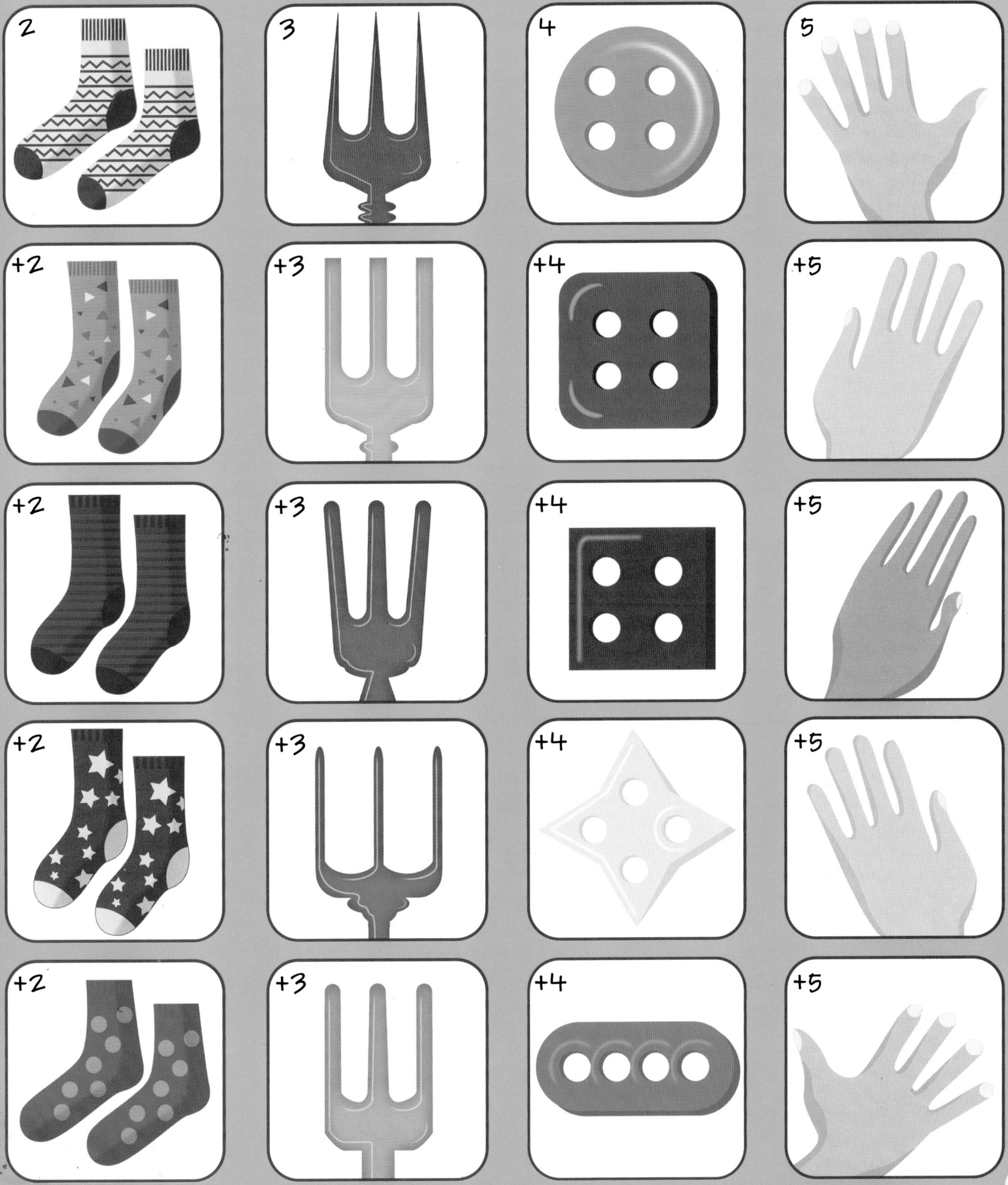

2

3

4

5

+2

+3

+4

+5

+2

+3

+4

+5

+2

+3

+4

+5

+2

+3

+4

+5

11

Maths machine

Are you ready for some maths magic? Then make special number cards called input, function and output cards, and build your machine. The function cards are your magic keys. They tell you what to do with the other numbers in this quick-moving calculation game.

Top tip

The number that starts the calculation is called the input. What happens to this number is the function. The output is the answer.

Make a maths machine

YOU WILL NEED
pen, coloured paper, big cardboard box, scissors

I'm the caller this time.

1 To make input cards, write the numbers 1 to 10 on sheets of green paper. To make output cards, write 2 to 15 on purple paper. To make function cards, write +1, +2, +3, +4, +5 on yellow paper.

2 To make your maths machine, ask an adult to help you cut off the top and one side of a cardboard box. Cut out windows like the ones in the big picture. Label them input, function and output.

HOW TO PLAY

◆ This game is for three people. There's a caller who is in charge and two players.

◆ First the caller lays out the input cards on one side of the machine and the output cards on the other. She hangs a function card in the middle window.

◆ Now the caller chooses an input card and hangs it in the first window.

◆ The players race to find the right output card and hang it in the output window. Whoever is first is the winner.

◆ Play the game three times then change the function. Who wins most often?

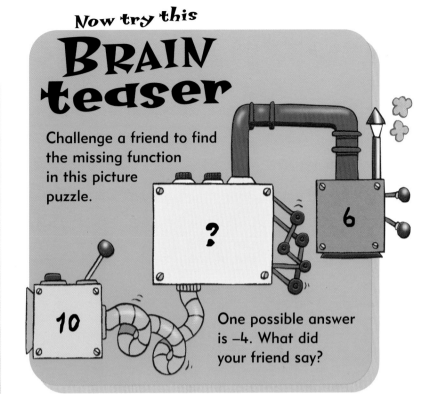

Now try this
BRAIN teaser

Challenge a friend to find the missing function in this picture puzzle.

One possible answer is –4. What did your friend say?

fold over the tops of the cards so they can hang from the windows

Number trails

Think of a number, any number! How many figures, or digits, does it have? Take the number 326. It has 3 digits. Say the number out loud. It has 3 hundreds, 2 tens and 6 units. The position of each digit helps you to work out the size of the number.

HOW TO PLAY

◆ First work out the number trails 1 to 5. Follow the logs or leaves, working out each part of the calculation as you go.

◆ Next, count each different type of animal in the picture. Which group of animals matches the total of which number trail?

HUNDREDS	TENS	UNITS
3	2	6
100		
100		
100		
there are 100 oranges in each crate	there are 10 oranges on each plate	these are single oranges

Travel the jungle trail

The long calculations, or number trails, on this page use 1, 2 and 3 digit numbers. Use a pen and paper to help work out the calculations.

3 → 900 → −100

2 → 4 → +3 → +13

1 → 60 → −40

Answers: 1) 3 snakes 2) 40 ants 3) 8 frogs 4) 6 toucans 5) 2 monkeys

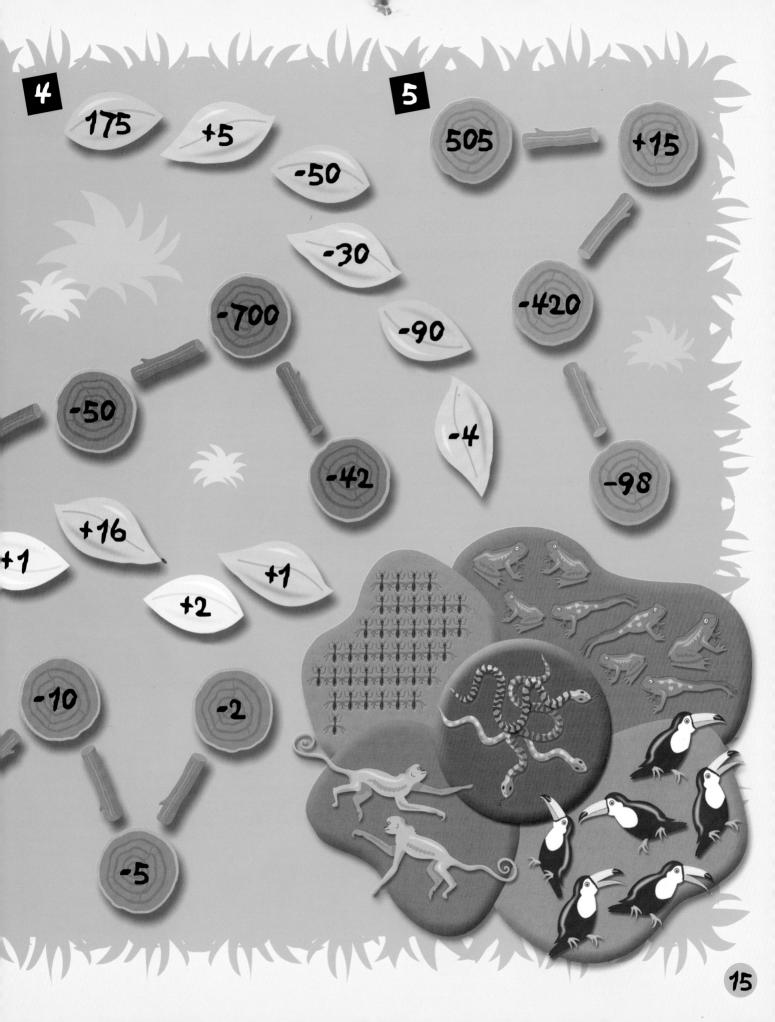

4

175 +5 -50 -30 -700 -50 -42 -90 -4 +16 +1 +1 +2 -10 -2 -5

5

505 +15 -420 -98

Odds, evens and halving

The fish game on this page is all about odd and even numbers and halving. An even number, such as 2, can be divided exactly in half. An odd number, such as 3, cannot be divided exactly in half. The fish here is blowing odd and even numbers. Look at the pattern the colours make.

even numbers are on the orange bubbles

odd numbers are on the blue bubbles

10 11 12
9   13
8   14
7   15
6   16
5   17
4   18
3   19
2   20
1

Make the odd and even fish cards

YOU WILL NEED
scissors, card, coloured pens, paper

1 Cut out 19 fish-shaped cards. Decorate them, then write the numbers 2 to 20 on them.

2 Now play the game. Shuffle the cards and put them number-side down on the table. Find a friend to play with and each pick up three fish.

3 Now for the tricky bit. You have to halve all even numbers and add one to all odd numbers. Check the blue and orange bubbles if you're not sure which number is odd and which is even. The picture below shows you how a game might work.

PROVE IT!

To find out if a big number is odd or even check the last digit. When it's odd, the whole number is odd. When it's even, so is the whole number. See how it works on the numbers here.

odd numbers	even numbers
2 3 3	1 6 2
4 6 7	5 7 8
7 8 5	9 0 6
odd number digits	**even number digits**

pick up a fish

STEP 1
halve 6 and you have 3

STEP 2
add 1 to 3 to make 4

STEP 3
halve 4 to reach 2

STEP 4
halve 2 to make 1 – this is the last step

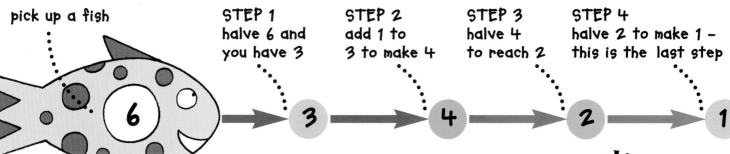

6 → 3 → 4 → 2 → 1

4 Both players work out how many steps it takes to reach number 1 for each fish. Whoever uses most steps wins. Play again using the remaining fish cards.

Now try this

BRAIN teaser

Challenge a friend to tell you if you get an odd or even number when you...

add even plus even?

4 + **2** = **6**

The answer is always even.

add odd plus odd?

5 + **3** = **8**

The answer is always even.

add odd plus even?

4 + **5** = **9**

The answer is always odd.

Counting sheep

Adding up lots of numbers quickly is helpful for all kinds of things, from puzzles and card games to tricky maths problems. Here's a sheep game to play. At the end you'll need to add up to see who's the winner.

PROVE IT!

It doesn't matter in which order you add up numbers. Check by working out the answer to the sum on the bottom washing.

Make the sheep game

YOU WILL NEED
coloured card, ruler, felt pen, scissors

.... this is a fence

1 Draw a board with five squares at the top and five down the sides. Make each square 6 cm.

2 Cut out 60 card fences. Each fence is 6 cm long and 1 cm wide. Cut out 25 squares, each measuring 4 cm. Draw a sheep with a number that's between 9 and 99 on each square.

18

3 Now play with a friend. Put a sheep on every square of the board. Then take turns to put down a fence. The player who completes a pen wins the sheep and takes it off the board. This player has another go.

4 At the end of the game add up the numbers on the sheep you've collected. The player with the bigger number is the winner.

BRAIN teaser

Challenge a friend to fill in this mystery square.

The numbers in each column, row and diagonal line must add up to 15. Here's a clue, use the numbers 1, 3, 7, 8 and 9 once each.

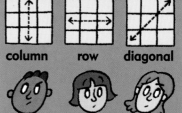

column   row   diagonal

Look at the finished magic square. The mystery is revealed! But check each line to make sure it adds up to 15.

8	3	4
1	5	9
6	7	2

Mystery numbers

Who can unravel the mystery of these number squares? First follow the steps to find out how to read them. Then keep your eyes open for hidden patterns in the numbers. These patterns are your clues. They will help you solve the missing numbers puzzles in the green and pink squares.

+	1	2	3
1	2	3	4
2	3	4	5
3	4	5	6

How to use the mystery squares

1 Look at the big number square on this page. The + sign at the top tells you it is an addition square.

2 Put a finger on number 2 on the top row of the addition square and a finger on number 2 down the side.

3 Run your fingers down and across the square until they meet. This number is the answer. Find the answers to the other additions in the square. Try doing it without using your fingers.

2 + 2 = 4

What's missing?

Work out the missing numbers for this addition square. Look at the numbers already in the square. Can you see the patterns they make? What might the answers be?

+	4	5	6
6	10	11	?
7	11	?	13
8	?	13	14

This next addition square uses bigger numbers. Work out the answers, then check them against the answer square below.

+	30	35	40
50	80	85	?
55	85	?	?
60	?	95	100

BRAIN teaser

In these puzzling squares, numbers become smaller and smaller. Challenge a friend to a guess-the-final-number game.

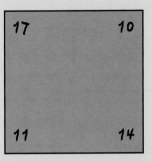

1. Draw a big square and ask a friend to give you 4 different numbers from 10 to 20. Write these in the square.

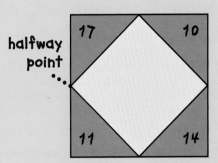

halfway point

2. Now mark the halfway points on your first square. Draw another square like the one shown above.

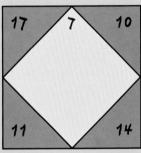

3. Take away the smaller number from the bigger number in the top two corners of the first square. Write in the answer.

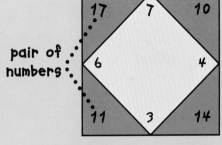

pair of numbers

4. Now look at the rest of the pairs of numbers. Take away the smaller numbers from the bigger ones. Write the answers in the second square.

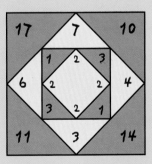

5. Carry on drawing smaller squares and finding the difference between the pairs of numbers.

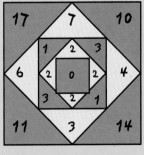

6. What's the final number? It's zero! Try the puzzle again using different numbers. Is the answer always zero?

Target practice

How good is your aim? Here's a chance to hit the high numbers. All you have to do is throw soft balls through holes in a target. Then with a little clever number work, you'll find the winner.

Make balls and a target

YOU WILL NEED
balloons, rice, funnel, scissors, large cardboard box, saucer, pen, tape, coloured paper

1 To make a ball, blow up a balloon and let out the air. Fill the balloon with rice and tie a knot to hold it in place. Cut the neck off another balloon and stretch it over the ball. Make two more balls in the same way.

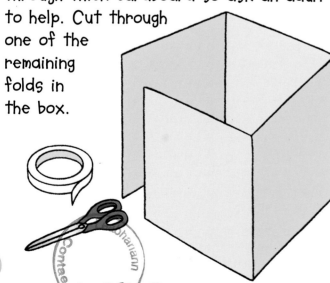

rice goes easily into the balloon if you use a funnel

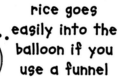

2 Now cut off the top and bottom of your box. It can be hard to cut through thick cardboard so ask an adult to help. Cut through one of the remaining folds in the box.

3 Flatten out the box. Then draw around a saucer to mark holes on one of the middle sections. Cut out the holes. Overlap the outside sections of the box to make a three-sided target. Fix in place with tape.

4 Write high numbers such as 56 and 250 on pieces of paper and tape them under the holes. Try changing the scores on the holes and see how this affects your aim!

decorate your target before you play

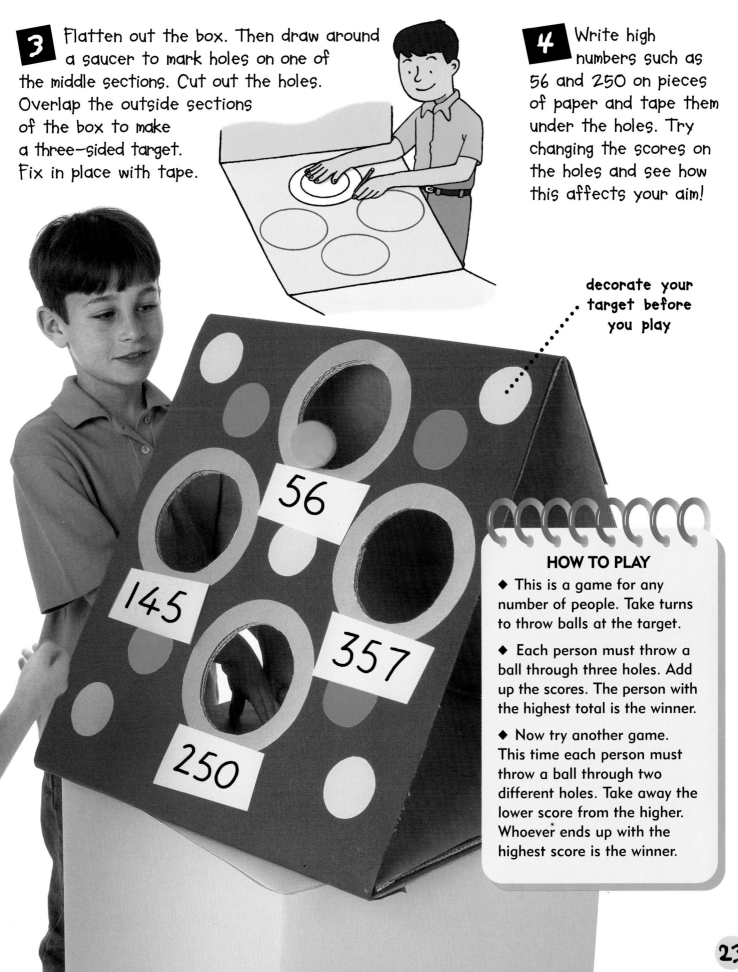

56

145

357

250

HOW TO PLAY

◆ This is a game for any number of people. Take turns to throw balls at the target.

◆ Each person must throw a ball through three holes. Add up the scores. The person with the highest total is the winner.

◆ Now try another game. This time each person must throw a ball through two different holes. Take away the lower score from the higher. Whoever ends up with the highest score is the winner.

Number tower

Now you know about adding and subtracting, you can play the number tower game. It's all about reaching the highest number possible in as few moves as you can manage. Follow the steps below to see how to play. Then add or subtract your way to a winning total.

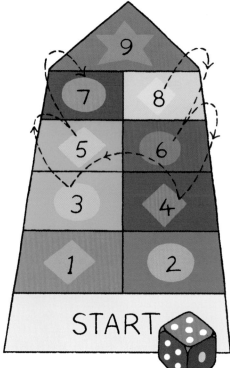

Play the number tower game

YOU WILL NEED
counters, one dice, paper, pen

1 Take turns to roll the dice. Move your counter the number of times it says on the dice. You can move in any direction, but must finish each go on the highest number possible. So if you roll a 4, you can jump 2, 4, 6 to land on 8. This makes your score 8.

2 Next go, let's say you roll 5. You can land on a number only once every turn. So start on 8 and jump 6, 4, 3, 5 to land on 7. Your score this time is 7. Add up your scores (8 + 7), to reach your total score of 15.

3 Carry on playing. Keep a check on your scores by writing them down. The first person to reach a total score of 50 is the winner.

4 Play the game again, but start with a total score of 50. Take away your score each turn. Who's first to reach zero?

play this game with a friend

24

play the number tower game on this board

counters go here to begin the game

PROVE IT!

The magical number 10 can actually make adding easier! See how it helps when you have to add 9 to a number.

Think of 9 as

9 +1 = 10

10 -1 = 9

So you add 27 + 9 like this

27 +10 = 37

37 -1 = 36

So 27 + 9 = 36

Remember, ten is the same as nine plus one.

Top tip

Remember, the number on the dice tells you how many places to move your counter. It doesn't tell you which number to go to on the board.

25

How many insects?

How many orange butterflies are there in the picture, but here's the catch, you can't count each one. Do you think there are five, or ten, or even twenty? To answer, you need to work out the number roughly. This is called estimating.

Make an estimating frame

YOU WILL NEED
card, ruler, pen, scissors, tape

1 Cut out 4 strips of card, 12 cm long and 3 cm wide. Lay them down so the ends overlap as shown in this picture. Tape the strips together.

PROVE IT!

Patterns and groups of objects can trick the eye. Look quickly at the apples. Are there the same number of apples in each group? Now count them. How close was your estimate?

2 Now use the frame. Hold it over the square with the blue border. There is 1 orange butterfly in this square. There are 12 squares, so an estimate of the total number is 1 added together 12 times. This means there are roughly 12 orange butterflies in the picture. Count to see how close this estimate is.

3 Estimate the number of wasps and ladybirds using your frame. Count each one to check your estimates. Now you can work out how many insects there are altogether.

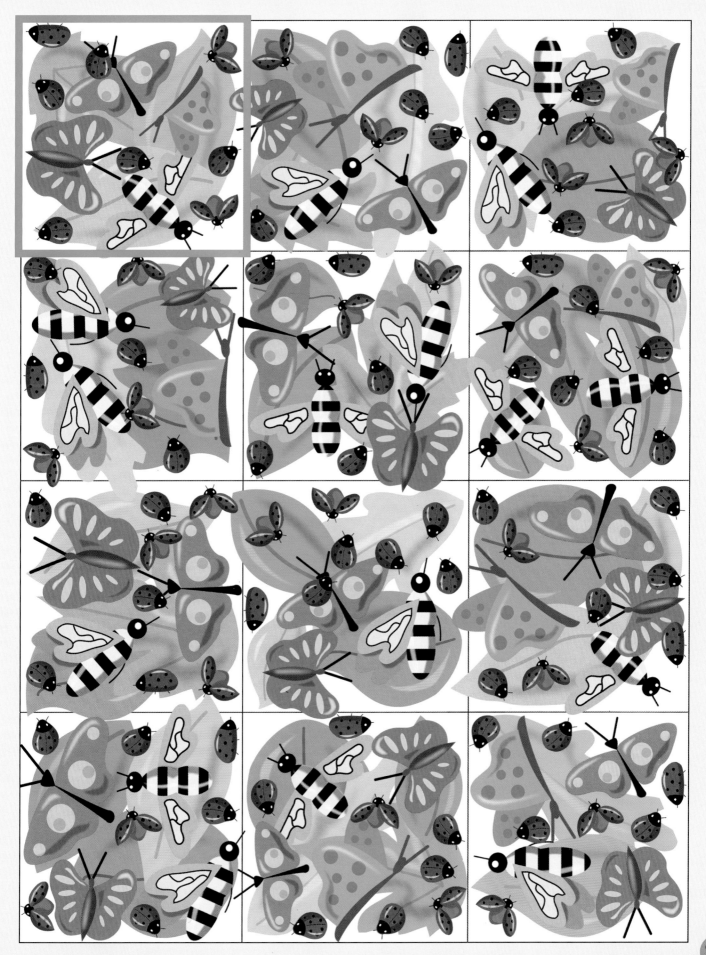

Think of a number

When you add and subtract, it's helpful to expect a particular answer. Then you know if your answer is likely to be right or wrong. The questions here have three possible answers. It's make your mind up time! Which answers do you expect to be right?

What's the likely answer?

3 How many goals are scored in a football match?

a 4

b 4,000

c 40,000

4 How much does a five-year-old weigh?

a 3 grams

b 23 grams

c 3 kilos

1 What age is a school student?

a 1

b 12

c 112

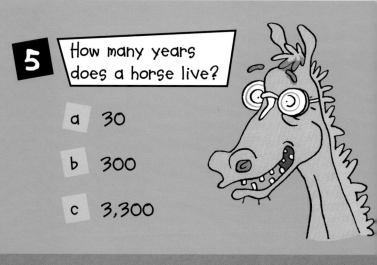

5 How many years does a horse live?

a 30

b 300

c 3,300

2 How many days are usually in a month?

a 3

b 30

c 300

6 How many times does your heart beat in a minute?

a 7

b 70

c 7 million

28

7 How many seconds are in a minute?

a 60

b 360

c 3,600

8 How many pages are in a book?

a 2

b 64

c 264,000

9 How many legs are on an insect?

a 6

b 6,000

c 60,000

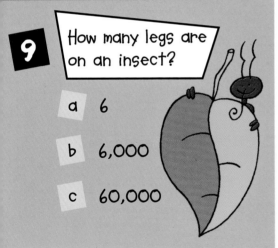

10 How many kittens are in a litter?

a 5

b 55

c 505

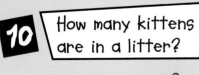

Number turnaround

When you change the order of digits in a number, you make a different number. Try it and see.

YOU WILL NEED
dice, pen, paper

1 Throw one dice three times and write down the numbers. Use these to make two and three digit numbers. For example, if you throw 3, 2, 6 you can make these 2 digit numbers 32, 23, 36, 63, 26 and 62.

2 Now write down your numbers in size order, starting with the smallest.

Smallest
23
26
32
36
62
63
236
263
326
362
623
632
Biggest

Now try this

BRAIN teaser

Challenge a friend to a guess-the-number game.

5

1. First ask your friend to think of a number from 1 to 10.

5+12
−2=15

2. Now ask her to add 12 to this number, then subtract 2.

15−5
=10

3. Finally ask your friend to take away the number she first thought of.

10

10

4. Tell her the number she ends up with is 10. Try the trick again. Can you see why the answer is always 10?

Useful words

add
The addition sign looks like this **+**. When you add numbers, you put them together to find a total. Here is an addition calculation.

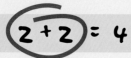

$$2 + 2 = 4$$

calculation
When you add or subtract numbers, you make calculations. Here are two calculations.

$$3 + 5 = 8$$
$$5 - 3 = 2$$

digit
The figures **0, 1, 2, 3, 4, 5, 6, 7, 8, 9** are all digits. They make up all the other numbers we use. The number **12** has two digits, so does the number **84**. The number **765** has three digits.

equals
The equals sign looks like this **=**. It means 'the same as'. What is on one side of the equals sign must always match, or balance, what is on the other side.

$$17 - 10 = 20 - 13$$

even number
Number 2 is an even number. Even numbers can be divided exactly in half. They happen every other number and make this pattern.

$$2, 4, 6, 8, 10...$$

function
This is the part of a calculation that tells you what to do. It connects two numbers or sets of numbers. Here the function is **+2**.

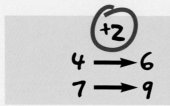

input
This is the number or numbers that start a calculation.

minus
This is the name of the **−** sign, which means to take away or subtract.

odd number
Number 3 is an odd number. Odd numbers cannot be divided exactly in half. They happen every other number and make this pattern.

$$1, 3, 5, 7, 9, 11...$$

output
The answer to a calculation is called the output.

pattern
When a series of numbers or shapes is repeated, it makes a pattern. Here are two patterns of numbers.

$$25, 35, 45, 55...$$
$$10, 9, 8, 7, 6, 5...$$

plus
This is the name of the **+** sign, which means to add or put together.

signs
In mathematics, signs are short ways of writing what is happening to the numbers in a calculation. Here are three signs.

subtract
The subtraction, or minus, sign looks like this **−**. When you subtract, you take one number away from another to find the difference. Here is a subtraction calculation.

$$10 - 6 = 4$$

Number pairs

Below are calculations that we use a lot. There are number pairs that add up to 10 and 20. There are also number pairs that are simple subtractions from 10.

10 + 0	=	10
9 + 1	=	10
8 + 2	=	10
7 + 3	=	10
6 + 4	=	10
5 + 5	=	10
4 + 6	=	10
3 + 7	=	10
2 + 8	=	10
1 + 9	=	10
0 + 10	=	10

10 − 0	=	10
10 − 1	=	9
10 − 2	=	8
10 − 3	=	7
10 − 4	=	6
10 − 5	=	5
10 − 6	=	4
10 − 7	=	3
10 − 8	=	2
10 − 9	=	1

20 + 0	=	20
19 + 1	=	20
18 + 2	=	20
17 + 3	=	20
16 + 4	=	20
15 + 5	=	20
14 + 6	=	20
13 + 7	=	20
12 + 8	=	20
11 + 9	=	20
10 + 10	=	20
9 + 11	=	20
8 + 12	=	20
7 + 13	=	20
6 + 14	=	20
5 + 15	=	20
4 + 16	=	20
3 + 17	=	20
2 + 18	=	20
1 + 19	=	20
0 + 20	=	20

Index

Notes for parents and teachers

This book helps children to gain confidence with numbers and calculations. Everyday life is full of calculations, from household accounts to pocket money. Being able to calculate is also a vital skill for many other mathematical topics.

Learning the language

To enjoy maths, children first have to understand the language of maths. This includes understanding words, such as 'adding', 'subtracting' and 'equals'. By working through this book, children can improve their maths vocabulary.

● Ask children how many words they can think of that mean the same as 'add', 'subtract' and 'equals'. Who can describe what these words mean?

Laying the groundwork

Quick recall is a basic ingredient for success with mathematics. Instantly knowing that $5 + 2 = 7$, $8 + 3 = 11$ or $10 - 4 = 6$ speeds up the whole mathematical process. Many ideas in this book help children to memorise simple calculations (look at pages 8, 9, 12, 13, 24 and 25). Here are a couple of other ideas for you to try.

● Use the fish made on page 16. Lay them face down on the table. Then pick up two. At the same time say 'add' or 'subtract'. Who can shout out the answer first?

● Change the target numbers on page 23 to numbers up to 20. Ask children to throw the balls through the holes. Then ask them to subtract their score numbers from 100. Who can reach zero or below in the fewest hits?

Number patterns

Help children look out for patterns in numbers. Odds and evens are simple number patterns. Adding a number to itself again and again forms another kind of pattern.

● Look at the number patterns in the mystery squares on pages 20 and 21. Ask children to tell you the next two numbers in each row and column.

● Use the number track on pages 6 and 7 to jump on in threes and fours. Ask children what the next numbers will be.

Using what's there

To solve number problems in everyday life, we sort out what's there and what's missing, work out a strategy and then go on to find a solution. Estimating is a particularly powerful strategy. Children can practise estimating when they try the activities on pages 26 to 29. They can also try this.

● Look quickly at the picture–addition chart on pages 10 and 11. Estimate the number of prongs on the forks and holes in the buttons. Count to check your estimates.

Taking part

To help build children's basic addition and subtraction skills, try to join in the games and activities in this book. Make the games as much fun as you can so the children will want to play them again and again.

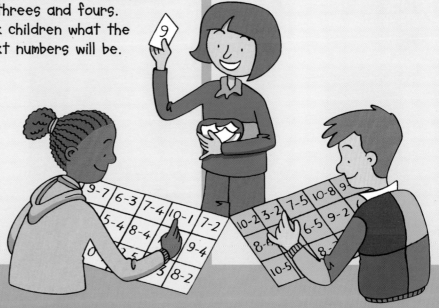